THE KELCE BROTHERS

A Little Golden Book® Biography

By Apple Jordan
Illustrated by Macky Pamintuan

🌼 A GOLDEN BOOK • NEW YORK

Text copyright © 2024 by Apple Jordan
Cover art and interior illustrations copyright © 2024 by Macky Pamintuan
All rights reserved. Published in the United States by Golden Books, an imprint of
Random House Children's Books, a division of Penguin Random House LLC, 1745 Broadway,
New York, NY 10019. Golden Books, A Golden Book, A Little Golden Book, the G colophon,
and the distinctive gold spine are registered trademarks of Penguin Random House LLC.
rhcbooks.com
Educators and librarians, for a variety of teaching tools, visit us at RHTeachersLibrarians.com
Library of Congress Control Number: 2024933951
ISBN 978-0-593-90428-2 (trade) — ISBN 978-0-593-90429-9 (ebook)
Printed in the United States of America
10 9 8 7 6 5 4 3 2 1

Jason Daniel Kelce was born on November 5, 1987. Two years later, on October 5, 1989, Travis Michael Kelce was born. The brothers grew up in Cleveland Heights, Ohio.

The Kelce family loved sports. Their dad, Ed, played football in high school, and their mom, Donna, won medals in the Junior Olympics for track and field. The family rooted for their hometown football team, the Cleveland Browns.

Jason and Travis started playing sports when they were very young. They learned to ice skate at the age of three and were in a youth hockey league. Their dad coached them in T-ball and baseball. They also enjoyed soccer and basketball.

They played football beginning in seventh grade.

The two brothers were always close. But they were competitive, too. Everything from wrestling matches in the backyard to racing to see who could get to the dinner table first was a chance to show who was best. Both boys liked to win!

At Cleveland Heights High School, Jason played hockey, lacrosse, and football. He was a captain of the football team his senior year.

He was also a musician and played the baritone saxophone in the school jazz band.

   While Travis was in high school, he played
basketball and baseball and was the quarterback of
the football team.
   Travis was a star athlete, but he wasn't always a
strong student. He failed French class and wasn't
allowed to play football his sophomore year. Jason was
disappointed. He was looking forward to being on the
same team as his little brother before going off to
college.

Raising two athletes wasn't easy. There was equipment to buy and schedules to keep track of, but Donna and Ed made it work. Often, one parent would see Jason play while the other would go watch Travis.

And they always had to have a fridge full of food because the boys would eat *a lot*. Sometimes, they would each have an entire chicken as a snack!

After high school, Jason went to the University of Cincinnati and made it onto their football team. He told his coaches all about his talented younger brother. Two years later, Travis got a football scholarship and joined Jason on campus.

Just as he did at home, Jason kept an eye on Travis and helped him do his best.

In 2011, Jason was drafted into the National Football League. He proudly played for the Philadelphia Eagles his whole career.

As the starting center on the Eagles offensive line, Jason snapped the ball to the quarterback to begin each play. He also blocked players on the other team from getting to the quarterback and told his teammates who they needed to block. He had to be tough, loud, and able to make quick decisions.

Jason received six first-team All-Pro honors and was selected to compete in seven Pro Bowls with other all-stars. He is one of the greatest centers to have ever played in the NFL!

During college, Travis switched positions from quarterback to tight end. He was drafted by the Kansas City Chiefs in 2013—two years after Jason went pro.

For his team jersey, Travis picked number 87 in honor of the year his big brother was born.

As a tight end for the Chiefs, Travis must be ready to catch passes from the quarterback and block players on the other team. He needs to be strong and fast!

Travis is one of the best tight ends in NFL history. He has set many records, including most postseason catches by any player and most postseason touchdowns by a tight end.

In 2018, the Eagles made it all the way to the Super Bowl. They were considered the underdogs, but Jason helped his team beat the New England Patriots, 41–33. It was the first time the Eagles ever won the Super Bowl!

Jason gave a memorable speech at the Super Bowl parade, wearing a traditional Philadelphia Mummers costume. He said the Eagles won because they wanted it more. "You know what an underdog is? It's a hungry dog!" he told the cheering fans. "Hungry dogs run faster!"

Travis got his chance at the championship two years later. In 2020, the Chiefs played the San Francisco 49ers in the Super Bowl. Travis scored one of three touchdowns in the last quarter of the game. The Chiefs won, 31–20.

Now both Kelce brothers were Super Bowl champs!

In 2023, Jason and Travis made NFL history by becoming the first brothers to play against each other in a Super Bowl! Mama Kelce wore a special Chiefs *and* Eagles jersey to support both sons. And she baked them cookies, just like she did when they were kids.

It was a close game, with the Chiefs beating the Eagles, 38–35. Jason was sad his team lost, but he was happy for Travis. After the game, the brothers hugged on the field.

Jason loves playing football, but the biggest joy of his life is his family. He and his wife, Kylie, have been married since 2018. They have three daughters, Wyatt, Elliotte, and Bennett. The girls love watching their dad play football and cheering him on. They also cheer for their uncle Travis—when he's not playing against their dad!

Travis and Jason never forgot the support they had growing up. They both started foundations to help other kids achieve their dreams, too.

Travis's Eighty-Seven & Running Foundation provides opportunities and resources for children across the country. Jason's (Be)Philly Foundation is dedicated to helping the kids of Philadelphia.

Jason also recorded two Christmas albums with his teammates and donated the money they made to charities. Jason even wrote one of the songs!

The brothers teamed up to host a podcast called *New Heights with Jason and Travis Kelce.* On the show, they talk about everything from football to family to their favorite food. They also chat with other famous athletes like Chiefs quarterback Patrick Mahomes.

In 2023, Travis started dating singer-songwriter Taylor Swift. Their fans loved seeing Taylor cheering at Travis's games alongside his friends and family.

When the Chiefs made it back to the Super Bowl in February 2024—and Travis helped his team beat the San Francisco 49ers in overtime—Taylor was there to help him celebrate his third championship win!

On March 4, 2024, after thirteen years in the NFL, Jason announced he was retiring. In an emotional speech, he said he wouldn't have accomplished what he did without the bond he and Travis share.

Jason Kelce and Travis Kelce are two of the greatest football players of all time. But more than anything else, they're brothers—and they will always be each other's biggest fan!